Chain of Poetic Tales

Green poetry

Ariel C. Cabasag

Ukiyoto Publishing

All global publishing rights are held by

Ukiyoto Publishing

Published in 2025

ISBN 9789370092259

www.ukiyoto.com

Dedication

I truly acknowledged publishing my poetry textbook. This is indeed an opportunity to explore the essence of the story, which could be found in every chain. Every person has different experiences in life, which might have turned into a tempest story. This book is not only talking about a story, but also, it transforms the essence of poetry, to bridge the people' lives.

In addition to that, this poetic tale attempts to urge people to look back to their past, for they could connect in down the road. Some of the chain may be miserable to you, especially if it could link to your past events in life. There are a few stories that awaken the people' eyes to how the downhearted life transformed into a better life. In short, this book could inspire readers to stay optimistic, despite the tragic stories that might have changed their lives. Similarly, people have faced different stories either awesome or ghast that could pull their hearts to carry the day.

This book can't be shared in the universe without the hands of Ukiyoto publishing company, which connects the story of poetic tales to the eyes of a trillion eyes. With that being said, I am forever thankful for accepting and making this poetic tale indelible, and making the content of the tales, as an undying chain, where it is worthwhile it useful as triumphant words as star in the peculiar stars.

Contents

Chain: Sonnet A
Fall In Love Thy Eyes

Trudging thy sand, sassy arms snugged the lamb
Shadow like the rain, often reaching my skin
O, irresistible eyes clip, like a honeyed psalm
Stood charismatic arts relieved my pain

What a French fries feelings, attached by the elegant eyes?
Thinking of you takes a wave
At summer season, skin often hunkered thy icy hand
Thinking of you, ocean turns a land
Milky-way and stars decried the secret Eden
Where I planted a true heaven

A giant cloud flocked the eyes and heart
Still, thy sight falling us apart
Whimsical night of a writing story
All day take you as my everlasting glory

Chain: Sonnet B
Undying Leaf

World filled with crazy drought
All days, hot wind squeeze thy leaf
No island survived, except flower fish
All nights, leaf stood like a fire
Till the tree endlessly tire

Every minute, wind burned the leaf
Still eyes painted the sun
Back the aisle, thousands of leaves trudge the sand
Endless, leaf quitted its games as deaf

While life carry the hilly chord
Leaf thirsts, still knows the Lord
Leaf is like a band singer
Thou life fills with ginger
In the end, rain makes
thy leaf sweeter

Chain: SONNET C
How thy feelings bridge us again

Often painted thee candied dove
Till I drenched at the Cambridge of love
Cloud nine raised the window of snow
Until aisle gripped us together,
So, waves pulled the beats river
Till right time unite us forever
Life intertwined the everlasting souls
To be found at honeyed hall
Where literature of feelings never dies
Indeed, English language exists like a book
Though wings fly beholding the other sky
Seeing the newly enchant whom you sigh
A million of rain bleeds till love gone Leaf of rose clipped us again
Meant to be, can be found the kingdom of Britain

Chain: Sonnet D
Undying Man

King of island haunted the plain grass
Till the house stood as ash
Thou Night filled a thousand dreams
Till uncountable folks graciously come
Eye behold thy death
Like Lord shimmed a truly violin of beat
War rugged the million of sands
And Earth tilt the holy land
Trees and lands thou gone
Except thy silver plant
Does trust and dip integrity
As heart sipped thy family
Death skipped to tap thy man
As Lord gave thy everlasting flies

Chain: Sonnet E
Holding You for a Million Nights

Withered leaf decried at thorny hills
As arms as free on the blued tales
Inveighed wings as invisible course
If dream house mightn't be yours
Heavy mountains fell the sea
As dead as the fantasy
Trillion nights dwelling the tunnel
Till swaying on the classy way
Where whiffed eyes fell down the flee
Often sparkled thy honeyed days
Tree sighs sauntered the hills to test
Cloying nights bonked the lovely sun
Often dwelled the exquisite brand
Like a beautiful eye undyingly sighs
West or east altered the sea
How drenched the alluring arms as bay
Invisible galaxy inflates with time
My love for you, forever rhyme

Chain: Sonnet F
Glimpsing at You for Million Nights

Fathom the day, a tantalizing eye caught me
Behold at your smile makes the day free
Though the world seems withered
Having you over my hands, a day turns to glittered
A cloying night to pull your shadow
Nevertheless, a silver eye drenched your window
Every night and day, a heart brimmed with your chords
In line with the honeybee, like clawed
Every night seems like a sea
Where my eyes gazed at your glee
Though you your irresistible appearance becomes dwindle
Letting you know clutch you like a kindle
A world looks like a bread
No matter where you are
Still a heart spare
Meeting you like a candied seed

Chain: Sonnet G
A Beautiful Night

A drenched night is flee of ethereal
Truly vivid with mellifluous caramel
As eyes as sunrise glimpse a cynosure
Often be thy cloying heart as pleasure
Every mile like a dulcet erstwhile
As endless eyes tilt as peace as sun
Till the plummed hands forever be land
Scintilla lagniappe shined the way
As Ariel's night seemed a seraphic tea
A night brimmed with sweetest cocophony
Like how thy night shed into a symphony
A sea night shud onto the bed
Till tantalizing eyes labyrinth the seed

Chain: Sonnet H
Endless Leaf

Rising Sun materialized over the lens
While feet slowly trudge filling motherly kin
Uncountable wind shook the thousands of trees
Till I fell down the beats
Thorny sunlight waved tree less
All nights pained thy storm till life ceased
Leaf is like a worthless man
Under the counter, the invisible mother forever care
Till the leaf eventually dared
Proven motherly love painted onto the sun
Leaf softly danced, as mother hand
Fire thoroughly cut the leaf
Under by a powerful coat
Loaf lived like a sweetest cave

Chain: Sonnet I
Bridge on the Aisle

Hearing your candied sounds
A pleasant night clutch by your lovely pounds
Seeing your gestures and enticing facial expressions
My eyes gripped by thy ravishing eyes;
Like how captivated thee communication
Every second, my mind never ceased to cast
Every smile I perceive, a hot feeling never lasts
Trudging the entire way
Your cloying shadow, look like a tray
The time to envision your inner feelings
The moments to slip back your special ceiling
Having an interpersonal
Like you were often original

Chain: Sonnet J
"Shining Star"

Waves of dull of eyes endless fluck
The truly bird luck
Beyond the hills,
Thousand clouds squeezed the man
Till it may be land
Green leaf concerted onto a stone
Still the man's name lies on the phone
Thorns never ceased the man
Till the sanguine golds lasts as pound
Life stood like a star
Thee messy eyes crop the far
Anyway, man flew as a galaxy
Where a truly success forever bee
Indeed, folks green-eyed monster
How he gripped the trillion stars

Chain: Sonnet K
Irresistible Snow

No day chuffed thy candied shine
All eyes trudged the windy rhyme
Endless nights swirled as a sword
Till the heart bleeded thy Lord
Thee rainbow rounded on west smile
Still stormy shook the feet as sigh
Life stood like a dead leaf
Zenith wind carry the shadow to uplift
Thorny tears ran like a river
How ceiling thy the sip forever
Feet often float till the sunset
Like how thy eyes be my asset
Uncountable breathes wooded thy snow
Invisible hand laddered like you do
Being you, million nights vividly as dream
Let's do the psalm of sweetest gleam

Chain: Sonnet L
Loving You till I Die

Loving you the most is like putting the elegant star
Glimpsing at you anytime, indeed afar
But putting you above my mind is like a guitar
Fathom the nights, love should never be scar
Endless the window at your aisle
Till a trillion of words forever sigh

Thy arms carry me amidst the rain
Thinking thy, clouds became a rainbow
Leaf fell to the green hand
Like irresistible feelings be your sun
A word can be erased, however love often belong
West and East hid the way
Still love lies the beauty of thy bay
Eternally, my love is like a song

Chain: Sonnet M
A Million Splendid Stars

Endless waves, the child ran like a wind
Till arrived to thy beauty of train
Dream seems like a garden
Where thy tireless hands made seeds
Whimsical feet strolled the million of hills
Often the sun faded the path
Still waves stood as a king
Life is filled with tallest mountain
Like how hurt floating above the tenth
Wind cut thy painful clouds
What the eyes glimpse at
A splendid of stars made a brightest dad
Life is like a shining star
Where never be afar

Chain: Sonnet N
A Teacher Lift Thousand Sands

A crystal eye clutched at the text
Two clouds intertwined endlessly at flexed
Undying night to shuddered while assessing the green test
Can't deny, an assessment withered the blued sea
Thy gazing at the treacly smile
Rapid lens thou made the test into a pie
Sunrise or storm, a student's heart seemed chuffed
Thy moment to clipped at the cough
A teacher sincerely revealed the test baraff
Thousand nights of hearing the whimpered
Not hitting the mean of the score appeared
In midst of, a superstar never beholds at their hands
Truly powerful the teacher, to bridge with their cands
End, thousands of wings hit the prolific pan
So, a teacher forever drenched to the sand

Chain: Sonnet O
Chances Happen Between Us

Love is like a book
How often I look
Clouds wrench us to breeze
still thy candied hands built a bridge
Days be a like coffin
Thy storm pulls us to bowfin
Amid the trillion of broken glasses
Storm served as stuff, to pass
Night is like an enticing heaven
Where a romantic story started again
Endless ceiling stood as feelings
Like how thy love gripped as my ring

Chain: Sonnet P
Often Loving You

Holding thy book like a bee
Under the sun I drenched at sea
The world makes me a ring
Had elegantly fled how I sing
Had beguiling lines enticed thou arms
Crossed the lines, bridge us onto crystal sun
Wherever you decried the pounds
The autumn thy enticing eyes
Till irresistible feeling flies
A lovely arm often alarms
Forever and ever, you're mine
King of sun rounded the may
Like how roses clipped at me
No ever feelings ran on the waves
Except thy cloying heaven behaves

Chain: Sonnet Q
Farewell to You

Seeing you is like a heaven
Where I've been waiting to leaven
A million nights seems not enough to forget
Though memory shud onto wet
Forever and ever, you are always my love
Sincere of words, be in my heart of dove
Couds can't be found in the sky
But I often think through cry
Like love truly hills thy wind
Till I notify you the change
A fathom night clipped us again
Love shed as thy Eden of salt
The path never hooks up the lane
To utter goodbye, hardly ends the pain

Chain: Sonnet R
Hills fall apart

Honeyed eyes lamped thy seas
Whimsical upbeat clouds more bees
Triumphant hills contemplate of you
Like the seed sweetly view
Undying leaf drenched the waterfall
Lovely hands painted the wall
Thunder eclipse cloyed the mountain How heart fell, as thy absence
No ever letters to heal the pain
Till relentless waves rummaged as lane
Whimsical nights envisioned of you
Yet, boundless sword blocked the sea
As thousands of tears fall away
Invisible river climbed the ravish hills
As enchant eyes brimmed the dark
When will you be back?
Lasts nights lovingly pack
Yet, swirled wind grip the land
Like how the eyes fell onto the sun
Two hills bridge the candied nights
Till eyes falling apart

Chain: Sonnet S

Love can't be change for you
Sunset covers the rhyming sun
Like ash may be gone
Trillion of clouds snowed thy ceiling
Till empty star falling
Loving you often sing
Like how the bees music cling
How I put the angel over the sea
Constant feelings be the day
Birds ran the sky
Like how feelings never die
Often, love connote the honeyed arms
Till eyes can see
Love be glowing tree

Chain: Sonnet T
Enticing feelings

Moon armed the thousand clouds
Like how eagle sazed crowd
Every eye pinned thy sea
Like how truly bee
How I far the sunset?
Under the sun makes me upset
Seeing the sunlight, melting onto part
Like how it drove thy heart
Oh star, how to be shined
Drenched by his enticing arms
Like how the volcano alarm
Till the sun blind
Seeing the hand, river never flood
How endless thy love?
Non-living thing forever exists
Like enticing feelings whist

Chain: Sonnet U
Mountain of Care

Sizzling of feelings fall
How heavy the star?
Empty can hardly fly
Like mother bird, often fry
Thunder plotted the tree
How hurt boughs, still a candy hand?
Often be thy band
Haven care could be free
Stop calling the silver rain!
Let the bessle of shore
Be the mountain of pure
Mirror how I bonked thy pain
If star fail hit the bay
A lovely seed lasts stay

Chain: Sonnet V
Seeing a Splendid Moon

Sees thy enticing shadow
How lovely thee window
Trudging on the hills
Lke gripping bough Pearly eyed whimsical bees
Till Andre seems the Eden peace
Eagle nipped the riddle song
Like how dazzling thee belong
Thinking of you takes a wave
Till splendid night looks a risen seed
Honeyed clouds ran the greened bell
How connotative thy fetching tale?
Tree exists by the sunlight
Seeing the candled sight
Where lasts eyed booked thy moon
A past lesson painted on thorny room

Chain: Sonnet W
Last Hug

Endless hills nipped thy cloying rainbow
Sunset flowed the moonlight
World looks like an empty cand
Yet, a lovely hand forever my brand
Rhythm of romantic lyrics lied above the nest
Like how thee hug and kiss
No ever metaphor seawed thy tintalating sow
Cinderela the seed, how the cap gripped the bustle
Till coquettish snow onto the enticing muscle
A day of falling the rain
Onto how mezereum heart the pain
Eyed on the west and east
Mind forever surmising in you
Till sun greened as true

Chain: Sonnet X
Death

Leaf lasts on May
Though river armed the frond
Like how ceiling edged on fall
O wind hold the brawl
Eyed hunkered the bee lips
How sun baffled the drenched leaf
A romantic scene can be written on the book
Though life exists on the molten invisible chrook
Dearest night be the fantasy
Where death can be found in the Noh
Romantic letters is still in you
Life pulled mountain onto a river
Where sobbing song belong
World like an empty can
Where death twisted on the sand

Chain: Sonnet Y
Purgatory

Dough the tides of lane
Sea lied on the beezle crane
Oh, unreturned loved
A season twitted onto a calve
Watered thy wings
How purgatory limb on the kings?
Will I'll be in City of Clean?
What if, love still unreturned
Let's love again!
But eyed blinded on the glenned
Dreaming of loving not hating
To pour thy roots of uncleaned

Chain: Sonnet Z
Heaven

Endless tears falling on thy lakes
How thy bawled the bough?
Sunset as salty memory
Like how the storm hid the foam
Life is a metaphor of star
Where heaven is never be scar
Fathom of love nipped the lovin
Eyed of enticing lines as violin
Invisibly bridging the purple love
In heaven, a dream feeling waved on dove
Oh! Staying the heaven like a sun
Till arms be my stun

BOOK 11
Sonnet 1 Forever in You

Trillion nights eyed thy plummet smile
Like how the goddess howled fly

Undeniably, eyed fancied in you
How the splendid sun splurged the bee
Our dreams, two shadows barrelled together
How relished nights handled forever?
Sun ripped the green bay
A honeyed moon sweeted thy day
How is the fate the ship?
Often pulling the waves till I sleep
Night is full of a bountiful tree
Where unfolded story as a glory

Sonnet 2
Ethereal Star

Thy lambency invisibly armed the key
Like how the clouds bonked the sea
Day and night pawed the palpable star
Till whimsy hands eyed afar
Million nights is like a seed
How the spunky the book to read?
Season of glee climbed the galaxy
As thee handed the hills till a fantasy
No letters nipped the cloying waves
Truly drenched by the resplendent aisles
Trudging the river thorns made me smile
Till a billion years, growth it as rhymes

Sonnet 3
A Thousand of Splendid Stars

Loveth of hills had truly pounds
Galaxy whiffed the spectacular sounds
Till the candied stars onto a hall
Every undying tear whirled a soul
A wicked day altered into a flawless bay
Where stars rhymed a fantastic song
Every line wrapped the nights till belong
Like how the sublime thy way
Snow nipped thy loveth of hills
Beneath the book
A written fantasy will close the window,
a star forever be the tea
Like an inveigle verse of thee
Stars danced as an angel glory
Till the epitome of art rhymed the world
Trudging the road is like Eden of chord
Where stars made a lovely story

Sonnet 4
Shadowing

Let thy wholly eyes inveigle cast
Till the clock whimsical feather as fast
Trillion of nights trudging on the sea
How idyll the research pigment as tea
Today, let the gleaming star fall FEU *students are longing to recall*
Blued eyes sleek the candied text
As Sir Ariel ran as stellar crest
Letters like a wave in the cave
Still, students the flawed upbeat
As often, mountain nipped thy sweet
Tranquil snow the austere sun
Like shrilling PR *subject seems fun*
It alters thy window as pounds
Till sunset hit onto thy luscious sound

Sonnet 5
I Am Still Be You

Seeing the pillow of thy enticing eyes
Shadow ran like a thunder turn me back
Sunset withered the roses as thy lack
Thousand nights dissolved the feelings
Yet, cloying memories never dies
Nights crossed the irresistible way
Yet, an arm never clutched at the sea wind shook like, how you pull me
Maybe dreams make us see
Anyway, beam rewrites thee nights
Where feelings pulled us again
Till heart can't feel the pain

LET ME REWRITE THE SEA

Oh, whimsical nights had made the bay into a tree! It's been a puppet brimmed with curled eyes and green-eyed relentlessly at me. Will I always be you? Akira's shadow fell on the lakes back it again into a day. Shall I be the sea? Million stars swirled the sea till painful hands falling on the bay. Will I carry on the bay? Glimpsing at the rain endlessly gripped the flame. Valentines day may happen again, yet love always be like a rain.

Oh, pellucid nights had made my rainy day into a fantasy. Akira slept over the clouds till rain fell her down to the aisles, where twilight gripped the sand. A night to depart the place, yet rain relentlessly grip the flame. A tempest night where Akira and Hassan triumphantly inveigled the nights, which made Akira a sunny day again. It took a trillion of nights of squeezing the bewitching nights till Hassan had faded, as part of her dreams. Portrayed with sewed nights, how Akira relentlessly squeezed the nights," love is like a wind, it will come, yet it fades," tears fell like a river over Akira's eyes.

That night, Hassan lived as non-human beings, due to alteration of Akira's feelings couldn't be a bay again.

What Akira could eyed the glass, the man portrayed with greened hills as germane as he was. As often, it painted into her memory. Couldn't deny, Akira couldn't alter the nights, unless she slept the sweetest land over the man's tale again. Due to Akira tears, it created an impeccable sea where Akira changed her life. Is Hassan still alive?

Over the hills, Hassan is still invisible, it's really opposite, what folks viewed. While Akira dwelled as a sea, full of hopeless dreams in dwelling by the ravishing tale. That night, Ariel, a secret wind, once he passed the sea, Akira's pain deleted on her memory. Ariel craved to reunite Akira and Hassan to have had a wonderful tale.

There was an enticing night, the wind passed the hills; thereafter the greened hills fall on the sea, where Hassan and Akira met again. It's a bountiful night of looking back their past, though Akira has been deleting, how she put her tales over him. Hassan craved to reunite their past, yet Akira often believed that love is like a wind, it will come, yet it fades again unexpectedly. Akira thanks to Ariel, how she survived the awful days. They put their hands together, still Akira's feelings can't be a bay again.

About the Author

Ariel C. Cabasag, LPT, MATELL

Ariel has been working as an English instructor and creative writer for almost six years in the Philippines. He's a man who loves letters and language, which really helps him to transform his imagination through creative writing. To him, life is meaningful and worthwhile, as he has expressed himself through writing such masterpieces in English language & literature.

In addition to that, he's a famous instructor in teaching English communication, which further drives him to showcase his talents in poetry and essay writing. Most of his students was really inspired by his talents; indeed, he has received many appreciation letters in teaching.

With regards to his educational background, he took MA in Teaching English Language and Literature at Ateneo University, where he further learned how to use the language dynamically. And he got idolized some effective professors, who indeed motivated him to tirelessly love teaching English language. After a year, he became a professor at Far Eastern University, where he published many poems: green letters in the cave and thousand splendid stars. Meanwhile, he started his second MA in Literary and Cultural Studies at Ateneo de Manila, where he further enhanced his talents in writing: to become globally competitive both writing career and teaching. Meanwhile, he took Juris Doctor program, as one of the famous Universities in the country.

To end, he lived his life with full of optimism and dynamism. He often aimed to put his story in the mirror, where society could take it as their lens, as people continuously dwell their lives.

www.ingramcontent.com/pod-product-compliance
Lightning Source LLC
LaVergne TN
LVHW041642070526
838199LV00053B/3509
* 9 7 8 9 3 7 0 0 9 2 2 5 9 *